Maurits Mouse and Rembrandt is a picture book published by Leopold in co-operation with the
Mauritshuis
Plein 29, 2511 CS Den Haag
www.mauritshuis.nl

Maurits Mouse has his own little mouse hole in the Mauritshuis. Can you find it?

For our two tiny mice

First print 2019

Translated by Marije Matthew
Design Studio Bos
Uitgeverij Leopold, Amsterdam | www.leopold.nl
NUR 217 | ISBN 978 90 258 7768 2

Ingrid & Dieter Schubert

Maurits Mouse and Rembrandt

The master and his mouse

Leopold, Amsterdam | Mauritshuis, Den Haag

Outside night has fallen, inside all is quiet.
It is time for Maurits Mouse to watch over the house again.
But first he is going to enjoy a nice, warm bath.
Suddenly he hears a rustling noise.

Worried, he climbs out of the water.
Four glistening eyes are looking out at him.
'No spying allowed,' Maurits calls out crossly.
'Sorry,' squeak two guinea pigs, 'but you have to come right away.'
With a heavy sigh, Maurits quickly gets dressed.

The friends jump down from their paintings.
'Have you heard, Maurits? Someone famous is coming to visit. And we're being hidden away in the basement. But we won't allow it! This is OUR house!'

Maurits Mouse clenches his fists: ‘I will protect you. Against any and all intruders!’
They walk through all the rooms together, looking in all the corners.
Suddenly Maurits spots something strange. A tiny hole in the wall beneath the old man!
‘What’s all this?’ Maurits cries out. ‘There’s only one mouse living here…
and that’s me!’

Maurits carefully sniffs at the hole. Then he wriggles his way through.
The other animals hold their breath. That Maurits would dare do such a thing, and in his best clothes!
'Help, I'm stuck!' Maurits squeaks.
His friends give him a shove and Maurits pushes off with both feet.
Suddenly he is shooting through an unfamiliar space faster than a rocket.
He tumbles, he turns, he falls and flies... He's not scared, he feels amazing.

Maurits lands in the middle of a sack full of flour.
Such a lot of dust, he thinks, a little confused.
He pats down his outfit and takes a look around.
Suddenly he is being lifted by his tail.
'And who's this little stylish mouse?'
Maurits clears his throat:
'I am Maurits Mouse, of noble birth!'

'And I'm Rembrant Harmenszoon van Rijn and I'm going to be a famous painter.'
Famous painter! What a show off! thinks Maurits.
'My father is a miller and my mother bakes bread,' says the boy. 'They won't allow any mice here, so watch out for the cat.
I'll look after you. But in return you'll have to pose for me. OK?'
Maurits nods. This boy is pretty funny.
But what was his name again? Rembrant Har something or other? Hmm, way too complicated.
'OK, Rem!'

Rem takes Maurits home with him, and puts him on a table in his room.
He closes the curtain and moves an oil lamp back and forth.
'I like things to be mysterious and exciting. First I look at the light and shadows from all angles. And I'll only start to draw once I'm happy with the effect.

Now sit still and look to the left...
Now to the right and lift your head a little...
No, don't wiggle your whiskers.'
Rem is pretty strict! And Maurits? He is having fun.

Early the next morning Rem has to go to school.
'Bonum Mane, Rembrandus,' says the school master.
'We have to speak Latin here,' whispers Rem.
'It just means Good Morning!'
During the lesson, Rem looks out of the window daydreaming. 'Can you see those people in the square, Maurits?
I'm going to paint them all. Because that's what I really want to do. Nothing else!
When are my parents finally going to understand that?'

When school is over, Rem and Maurits go out and explore the city. They play hide and seek behind the pillars in the large church. Rem makes sketches wherever he goes.

Rem also draws himself. He loves to dress up and pull funny faces.
Maurits has to hold the mirror up for him.
Rem makes himself look happy, serious or sad. 'Guess how I'm feeling now?'
Maurits always gets it right.
'You are my first pupil, Maurits. But later I'm going to have a house full of them!'
'You're getting too big for your boots, Rem!'

Maurits learns how to sharpen a quill.

And he mixes the ink
like an expert artist.

Maurits is allowed to draw too.
Which is much harder than he
thought!

Rem practises his signature a lot.
Once when Rem is not looking, Maurits quickly adds a new letter between two of the others. That looks better!

One evening when they are sitting by the water, Rem says happily: ‘Can you see that white house? That’s where I’m finally allowed to go and learn how to paint from a master.’
Then he looks sad. ‘But you can’t come with me.’
‘That’s OK,’ Maurits says, ‘it’s time to go home. They’ll be missing me terribly.’

‘Where are you from?’
‘From another time, far, far away. I flew through time and space quicker than a rocket to get here.’
Rem looks at him in surprise. ‘Rocket? Flew? Time and space? What kind of story is that?’

Maurits takes Rem back to the mill and points to the tiny hole.
'Only I can fit through. You'll have to give me a push.'

‘Wait a moment,’ Rem laughs. ‘You’ve got quite the imagination, but just in case, I’ll give you something of mine to take with you. For later, when I’ve been really famous for ages! Ha ha.’
Silly Rem.
Maurits gives him a gentle mouse kiss and then wriggles back through the hole.
‘Now, Rem!’
Rem gives a good push with his finger.
And once again Maurits tumbles, turns, falls and flies. It feels like the blink of an eye, and yet weightless and never-ending at the same time.

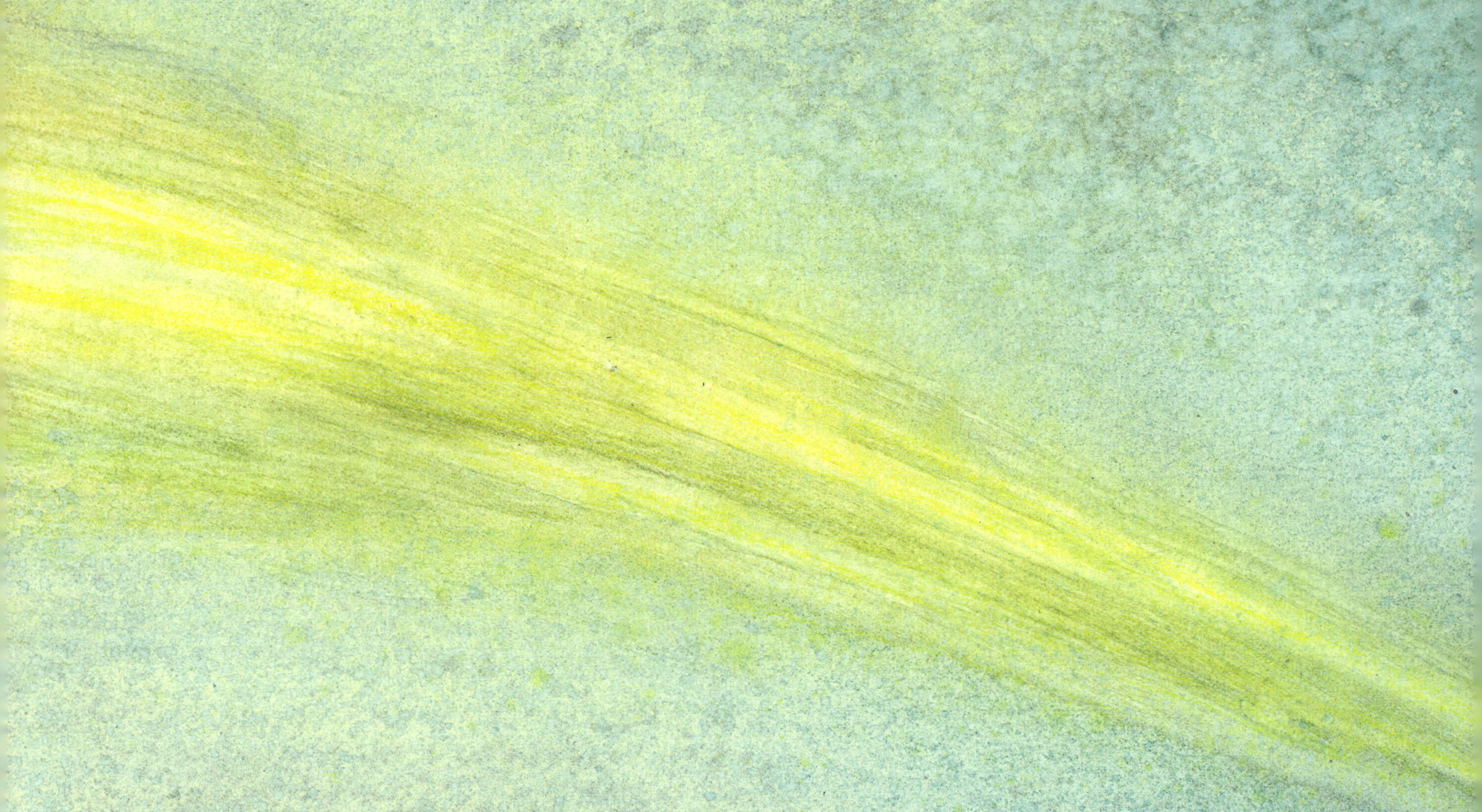

All of a sudden, Maurits lands back between his friends with a thud.
‘Where have you been?’ the guinea pigs ask.
‘Was I gone for long?’ he asks feeling dizzy.
‘Not too long.’
Maurits stands up and looks around.
Everything is as it always was. But wait!

There, in the corner… are some paintings he has never seen before.
The guinea pigs whisper mysteriously:
'The guest has already been. Luckily none of us have to go to the basement.
They're paintings by a Rem… or Ruben… something like that.'

‘Rembrandt,’ sighs Maurits.
He’s holding something tightly in his hand.
A lock of hair.
Which he will treasure. Now and forever.